AMERICA'S SONGS

MY COUNTRY —'Tis of— THEE

Cavendish Square
New York

KATE SHOUP

Published in 2020 by Cavendish Square Publishing, LLC
243 5th Avenue, Suite 136, New York, NY 10016

First Edition

Website: cavendishsq.com

Library of Congress Cataloging-in-Publication Data

Names: Shoup, Kate, 1972- author.
Title: My country 'tis of thee / Kate Shoup.
Description: First edition. | New York : Cavendish Square, 2020. | Series: America's songs | Includes bibliographical references and index.
Identifiers: LCCN 2018060543 (print) | LCCN 2018060632 (ebook) | ISBN 9781502648723 (ebook) | ISBN 9781502648716 (library bound) ISBN 9781502648693 (pbk.) | ISBN 9781502648709 (6 pack)
Subjects: LCSH: Smith, Samuel Francis, 1808-1895. America--Juvenile literature. | Patriotic music--United States--History and criticism--Juvenile literature.
Classification: LCC ML3561.A5 (ebook) | LCC ML3561.A5 S56 2018 (print) | DDC 782.42/15990973--dc23
LC record available at https://lccn.loc.gov/2018060543

Editorial Director: David McNamara
Editor: Kristen Susienka
Copy Editor: Nathan Heidelberger
Associate Art Director: Alan Sliwinski
Designer: Joe Parenteau
Production Coordinator: Karol Szymczuk
Photo Research: J8 Media

The photographs in this book are used by permission and through the courtesy of: Cover Skreidzeleu/Shutterstock.com; p. 4 Adam Springer/iStock/Getty Images; p. 6 transcribed by Dr. Nathan Heidelberger; p. 8 The Print Collector/Getty Images; p. 10 Johns Hopkins University Sheridan Libraries/Levy/Gado/Getty Images; p. 12, 27 Hulton Archive/Getty Images; p. 14 Albert Bierstadt/Metropolitan Museum of Art/Bridgeman Images; p. 16 Lowell Mason Foundation/Digital Commonwealth; p. 17 Rainer Lesniewski/Shutterstock.com; p. 18 Buyenlarge/Getty Images; p. 19 DeAgostini/Getty Images; p. 22 Helen H. Richardson/The Denver Post/Getty Images; p. 24 Fred Prouser/Reuters/Newscom; p. 25 (top, bottom) Francis Miller/The LIFE Picture Collection/Getty Images, Alex Wong/Getty Images; p. 26 Mark Wilson/Getty Images.

Printed in the United States of America

CONTENTS

America's natural beauty inspired the words for "My Country 'Tis of Thee."

CHAPTER 1

A Great American Hymn

America's national **anthem** is "The Star-Spangled Banner." However, this was not always true. "The Star-Spangled Banner" didn't become the national anthem until 1931. Before that, Americans sang different songs to celebrate their country. One of these songs was "My Country 'Tis of Thee."

My Country 'Tis of Thee

Lyrics by Samuel Francis Smith

My native country, thee,
Land of the noble free,
Thy name I love;
I love thy rocks and rills,
Thy woods and templed hills,
My heart with rapture thrills,
Like that above.

Let music swell the breeze,
And ring from all the trees
Sweet freedom's song;
Let mortal tongues awake,
Let all that breathe partake,
Let rocks their silence break,
The sound prolong.

Our fathers' God, to Thee,
Author of liberty,
To Thee we sing;
Long may our land be bright,
With freedom's holy light,
Protect us by Thy might,
Great God, our King.

FACT

A children's choir in Boston, Massachusetts, was the first to perform the song. They sang it on July 4, 1831.

"God Save the King"

The **melody**, or tune, for "My Country 'Tis of Thee" is the same one used for an older English song called "God Save the King [or Queen]." The words to "God Save the King" honor the king (or queen) of England. Historians are not sure

The words to "God Save the King" were written to honor King George II of England, pictured here.

who wrote "God Save the King." However, they do know the song was first published in England in 1744. It honored King George II.

New Words for an Old Tune

In 1831, a student from Massachusetts named Samuel Francis Smith wrote new **lyrics**, or words, for "God Save the King." Smith was twenty-four years old. He called his new song a **patriotic hymn**. He named it "America." Later, the song's name changed to "My Country 'Tis of Thee." Smith wrote more than 150 songs in his life.

Americans liked "My Country 'Tis of Thee." It became a song that defined America. People sang it in church and at ceremonies and celebrations. Today, the song is still important to many Americans.

FACT

It took Smith just thirty minutes to write the lyrics for "My Country 'Tis of Thee."

This is the cover for a version of the sheet music for "My Country 'Tis of Thee" printed in 1898. Its bright colors and drawings signal that the song is patriotic.

What Does It Mean?

“My Country ’Tis of Thee” is about Smith’s love for America. The song begins by honoring the country’s past: “Land where my fathers died, / Land of the Pilgrims’ pride.” Then the song celebrates the country’s beautiful nature. It talks about America’s **landscape**. Finally, the song asks God to protect America: “Protect us by Thy might, / Great God, our King.” Within the song, there are many old-fashioned words. Once you know their meaning, you can understand the song better.

Words to Know

might Another word for strength.
partake To take part in something.
rapture A feeling of extreme happiness.
rills Small streams.
thee An old form of the word “you.”
thy An old form of the word “your.”
’tis A combination of the words “it” and “is.”
tongues Another word for languages.

This is a portrait of Samuel Francis Smith, the man who wrote the words to "My Country 'Tis of Thee."

CHAPTER 2

The History of the Song

The story of "My Country 'Tis of Thee" starts in 1831. That year, an American music teacher named Lowell Mason found some music books from Germany. Mason asked his friend to translate the music books into English. The friend was Samuel Francis Smith. Translating the songs inspired Smith to write "My Country 'Tis of Thee."

Smith's Inspiration

One of the songs Smith translated was called "God Bless Our Native Land." The **theme** of the song was God protecting the country. It had the same melody as "God Save the King." "God Bless Our Native Land"

America's beautiful scenery inspired artists and musicians during the Romantic era. This painting shows a landscape from Yosemite in 1866.

inspired Smith to write new words for the melody, but about America. The song became "My Country 'Tis of Thee."

Smith lived at a time when America was changing. The country was growing. People explored parts of America that had not been explored for a long time. Some people were moving to new parts of America. They liked to see America's beautiful forests, mountains, and rivers. People who enjoyed nature and wanted to protect it were called Romantics. What they believed in was called Romanticism. Romanticism inspired Smith to add the theme of America's natural beauty to his new song.

An Anthem for Change

Lowell Mason read the words to Smith's song. He liked them. He had his choir sing the song at a

Dr. Lowell Mason was a music teacher. He was a friend of Samuel Francis Smith.

children's church service. People liked the words to the song and started to sing them. Soon, the song became one lots of people enjoyed.

The song's words have been changed in different parts of history. In the 1800s, the new words usually talked about slavery. That's because many Americans owned slaves. Most slaves lived in the South. In 1843, an **abolitionist** named A. G. Duncan added new verses to **protest** slavery.

From 1861 to 1865, America fought a war between North and South. The war was fought over slavery.

It was called the Civil War. In 1861, a Southerner named George Henry Miles changed the words to celebrate the South. Miles called his song "God Save the South." It became a popular song

> **FACT**
> The national anthems for Great Britain, New Zealand, and Liechtenstein have the same melody as "My Country 'Tis of Thee."

This map shows the United States at the beginning of the Civil War in 1861. Red states supported slavery. Green states were against it. Yellow states had slaves but supported the North. Purple areas were not yet states.

In 1863, President Abraham Lincoln wrote the Emancipation Proclamation to free the slaves. This illustration shows Lincoln surrounded by the proclamation.

for Southern soldiers to sing during the Civil War. In 1863, the song's words were changed again to celebrate when President Abraham Lincoln freed the slaves living in the United States.

People have rewritten "My Country 'Tis of Thee" to talk about many other things too. Some examples are workers' rights, women's rights, and equality for Native Americans.

FACT

Smith added new words to the song in 1889. This was one hundred years after George Washington became president. The new verse was in honor of Washington becoming president.

George Washington was a great military leader and president.

Timeline

- **1744** The melody for "God Save the King" and "My Country 'Tis of Thee" is printed in England.
- **1776–1783** The American Revolution happens.
- **1831** Samuel Francis Smith writes "My Country 'Tis of Thee."
- **1843** A. G. Duncan adds antislavery words to Smith's song.
- **1861–1865** The American Civil War takes place.
- **1861** George Henry Miles rewrites Smith's song and renames it "God Save the South."

- **1863** New verses are added to Smith's song to celebrate the freeing of the slaves.
- **1883** Elizabeth Boynton Harbert rewrites Smith's song to push for women's rights and renames it "The New America."
- **1889** Smith adds a new verse to the song to honor George Washington.
- **1891** Smith's song is made into a protest song to push for workers' rights.
- **1914–1918** World War I happens.
- **1919** A woman named Red Bird rewrites Smith's song and renames it "The Red Man's America" to push for rights for Native Americans.

This boy scout is singing during a Fourth of July parade in Colorado in 2016. Americans often sing "My Country 'Tis of Thee" during patriotic ceremonies.

CHAPTER 3

"My Country's" Legacy

Today, people are proud of the song "My Country 'Tis of Thee." Many people know its words. They sing it or listen to it during celebrations or for special holidays, like on the Fourth of July. Sometimes churches play it during services. Marching bands play the song too.

FACT

After attacks on **September 11, 2001**, a famous band called Crosby, Stills and Nash sang "My Country 'Tis of Thee" on television to unite Americans.

Stephen Stills (*left*) and Graham Nash (*right*) sing the song on *The Tonight Show* after the 9/11 attacks in 2001.

A Proud Patriotic Song

The song means a lot to people. Some people like it so much they want it to be another national anthem. Even though "My Country 'Tis of Thee" is not America's national anthem, it is still a popular patriotic American song.

Protest Song

Many people in history have sung the song or used its words. For example, during the 1960s, people sang "My Country 'Tis of Thee" to stand up for equal rights for African Americans. In 1960, students from Alabama State University sang the song on the steps of the Alabama State Capitol in Montgomery. In 1963, Dr. Martin Luther King Jr. spoke some words from the song in his famous "I Have a Dream" speech.

Dr. Martin Luther King Jr. delivers his "I Have a Dream" speech in 1963.

Celebrations and Ceremonies

Today, Americans sing "My Country 'Tis of Thee" during Fourth of July parties and parades. Americans also sing "My Country 'Tis of Thee" during political events. For example, a famous singer named Aretha Franklin sang the

Aretha Franklin sings at the inauguration in 2009.

> **FACT**
> Singer Kelly Clarkson sang the song at President Obama's second **inauguration** in 2013.

song when Barack Obama became president in 2009.

Finally, the song is sometimes sung during funerals. In 2018, it was sung at Senator John McCain's funeral.

No matter where the song is sung, people like it. The song means something to everyone. It helps people and makes them feel glad for America.

The funeral service for Senator John McCain in 2018 featured the song.

Marian Anderson and the Lincoln Memorial Show

Marian Anderson sings in front of the Lincoln Memorial in 1939.

Marian Anderson was a famous African American singer. In 1939, she planned a performance in Washington, DC. Her show was to take place at a theater called Constitution Hall. The group in charge of the hall canceled the show because Anderson was African American.

Anderson decided to perform somewhere else. She chose the Lincoln Memorial. More than seventy-five thousand people came to hear her sing. Millions more listened to her on the radio.

Anderson started her show by singing "My Country 'Tis of Thee." This was to protest the decision to **bar** her from Constitution Hall. Her performance was very powerful. It is one of the best performances of the song ever recorded.

GLOSSARY

abolitionist A person who pushed for an end to slavery.

anthem A song sung by a particular group or for a specific cause.

bar To stop someone from doing something.

inauguration The ceremony that happens when a person becomes president of the United States.

landscape The natural features of a place, like trees, mountains, and lakes.

lyrics The words of a song.

melody The main part in a piece of music that people sing.

patriotic hymn A song that talks about loving a person's country.

protest To speak out against something.

September 11, 2001 The day when terrorists attacked New York City and Washington, DC. Many people died.

theme The main idea of a song, book, or poem.

FIND OUT MORE

Books

Murphy, Claire Rudolf. *My Country 'Tis of Thee: How One Song Reveals the History of Civil Rights*. New York: Henry Holt and Co., 2014.

Ouren, Todd. *America: My Country 'Tis of Thee: An American Song About Freedom*. Minneapolis: Picture Window Books, 2003.

Wesolowski, Harriet. *The Songs We Sing: Honoring Our Country*. New York: PowerKids, 2012.

Website

Patriotic Songs

https://kids.niehs.nih.gov/games/songs/patriotic/index.htm

Visit this website for lyrics to several patriotic songs—including "My Country 'Tis of Thee."

Videos

Aretha Franklin Sings at Obama's Inauguration

https://abcnews.go.com/Archives/video/aretha-franklin-sings-obamas-inauguration-57189714

This video shows Aretha Franklin's performance of "My Country 'Tis of Thee" during President Obama's inauguration in 2009.

Marian Anderson Sings at Lincoln Memorial

https://www.youtube.com/watch?v=mAONYTMf2pk

This video shows Marian Anderson's performance of "My Country 'Tis of Thee" at the Lincoln Memorial in 1939.

INDEX

Page numbers in **boldface** refer to images. Entries in **boldface** are glossary terms.

ABOUT THE AUTHOR

Kate Shoup has written more than fifty books and has edited hundreds more. When not working, Shoup loves to travel, watch IndyCar racing, ski, read, and ride her motorcycle. She lives in Indianapolis with her husband and their dog.